THE VALUE OF SAVING

The Story of Benjamin Franklin

VALUE COMMUNICATIONS, INC.
PUBLISHERS
LA JOLLA, CALIFORNIA

THE VALUE OF SAVING

The Story of
Benjamin Franklin

BY SPENCER JOHNSON, M.D.

THE DANBURY PRESS

The Value of Saving is part of the ValueTales series.

The Value of Saving text copyright © 1978 by Spencer Johnson, M.D.
Illustrations copyright © 1978 by Value Communications, Inc.

First Edition
Manufactured in the United States of America
For information write to: ValueTales, P.O. Box 1012
La Jolla, CA 92038

Library of Congress Cataloging in Publication Data

Johnson, Spencer.
    The value of saving.

    (ValueTales series)
    SUMMARY: A brief biography of the outstanding
eighteenth-century printer, inventor, and statesman,
emphasizing the value of saving in his life.
    1.   Franklin, Benjamin, 1706-1790—Juvenile
literature.   2.   Statesmen—United States—
Biography—Juvenile literature.   3.   Saving and
thrift—Juvenile literature.   [1.   Franklin,
Benjamin, 1706-1790.   2.   Statesmen.   3.   Saving
and investment]   I.   Title.
E302.6.F8J56   973.3'092'4   [B]   78-8652

ISBN 0-916392-17-1

This tale is about a thrifty and inventive person, Benjamin Franklin. The story that follows is based on events in his life. More historical facts about Benjamin Franklin can be found on page 63.

Once upon a time...

in the days when our country was still a British colony, a little boy named Ben Franklin lived in Boston with his mother and father.

Ben was a bright, busy lad. He liked to read and to tinker with things. He also liked to play with his friends and to find out about how things work.

One day, when he was eight years old, he said to himself, "I'm going to have some fun. I'm going to invent a way to save time so I'll have more of it."

When he finished his invention, Ben set out to show it to his friend Tom. On the way he saw a rich man drop a penny in the street.

"Sir!" cried Ben. "You dropped your penny."

"Why so I did," said the man. "You're an honest boy. Just for that you may keep the penny."

"Thank you, sir," said Ben. "I'll keep it and save it, so that I'll have it when I need a penny for something important."

"That's a wise idea," said the man, and he went on his way.

Ben rubbed the penny between his fingers. It felt wonderfully smooth. He flipped it into the air. "You're really a special penny," he announced. "I may decide to save you forever!"

When he said that, something very strange happened.

As the penny flipped end over end, Ben thought he saw a smiling face on the coin. It seemed to him that the penny was talking, saying, "Hi there, Ben. I'm Benny the penny!"

The little boy was startled for a moment. But then he laughed. He knew that pennies couldn't talk. He knew that when he heard Benny, he was really listening to himself.

Don't you sometimes talk to yourself this way?

Ben thought it was fun. He decided he'd do it some more, and he made believe that Benny the penny said, "What are you thinking right now, Ben?"

"I'm thinking about you, Benny," said Ben with a laugh. "I'm thinking I may save you because you're such a special penny. And I'm thinking about my invention, too. Won't my friend Tom be surprised when he sees it!"

"What is your invention?" Benny asked.

"It's a Time-Saving Swimming Machine," Ben answered. He spoke in a way that made him sound very important. Then he laughed. "Come on, Benny, and see for yourself," he invited.

Ben tucked Benny the penny into his pocket and hurried on to his friend's house. "Tom, look at this," he said when he got there. "It's my new swimming machine."

"Swimming machine?" said Tom. "It doesn't look like much of any kind of machine to me. How does it work?"

"I put my thumbs through these holes," Ben explained. "Then I can swim very fast, because the boards are like paddles on my hands."

"Let's see you do it," said Tom. "I'll race you across the pond!"

So Tom and Ben raced. And who do you think won? Why Ben did.

"Say, that really *is* a super invention," said Tom. He didn't know it, and neither did Ben, but some day someone else would invent a device that worked like Ben's wooden paddles—rubber fins for swimmers' feet.

"Do you want to see something else I thought of?" asked Ben.

Ben picked up the kite he had brought. He ran along beside the pond until the kite was flying high in the wind. Then he jumped into the water, holding fast to the kite string.

"What in the world are you doing?" asked Tom.

Benny the penny wondered, too. But then he saw Ben simply floating in the water while the kite pulled him faster and faster until he reached the far end of the pond.

"Isn't this a great way to save time?" cried Ben. "And energy, too! I got here in seconds, and I didn't have to move a muscle to do it!"

"I don't know about saving time and energy," said Tom, "but that sure looks like fun!"

It was fun. Ben had lots of fun when he was a boy. But before he was very old he had to go to work, and work hard.

What sort of work do you think he did?

15

He was an apprentice in the printing shop owned by his older brother James.

In colonial days, many boys learned a job by working as apprentices. Ben loved books, so when he was ten years old his mother and father decided that he could be James's apprentice. As a master printer, James was to teach Ben all about printing. He also promised that Ben would have a room to sleep in and plenty to eat. In return for this, Ben was to work for James without any pay until he was twenty-one years old.

Of course, Ben's parents hoped that James would take good care of Ben, and would be fair and kind to the young apprentice. But things did not work out so happily. True, James taught Ben to be a good printer, and Ben did work hard. But Ben learned so quickly that James became a bit jealous. And after a while Ben grew tired of working without pay.

"I feel so helpless when I don't have any money," said Ben one day to Benny the penny. "I feel as if I don't have any control over my own life."

Then Ben thought of a way to earn money in a very clever way.

Ben didn't like mealtimes at James's shop. Everyone ate together, and Ben's plate was often much too full of things he didn't like or need. He decided that he would rather eat by himself and have the kind of food he enjoyed—and he figured out how he could do this and get money, too.

"James," he said, "if you'll give me just half the money you usually spend for my food, I'll buy my own."

James quickly agreed to this, and Ben took the little bit of money that James gave him. He spent half of it for the food that he really needed to eat, and he saved the other half for himself.

"This is pretty nice, isn't it?" he said to Benny, as he ate alone in his room. "I'm having just what I want for dinner, and at the same time I'm saving money for some special things."

Ben was terribly proud of himself, and there's nothing wrong with that. Aren't you ever proud of yourself when you do something clever?

Now Ben knew that life was more than just a good dinner and a room of his own. So he used some of the money he saved to buy books that he wanted to read. "Books are like food for your brain, Benny," he said, and he spent every minute that he could reading.

To get the most for his money, Ben would often buy a book, read it, then sell it to buy another. But if it was a book he wanted to read more than once, he would keep it. And no matter how many books he bought, he always managed to save some of his money.

"If I set something aside, it will be there later when I need it," he said. "That makes me feel grown up. It makes me feel as if I'm more in charge of myself."

"You may be young," said Benny, "but you know a lot about saving. I hope you save me, and don't spend me by mistake. I want to be here when you grow up, to see how things turn out for you."

Ben laughed. "How could I spend you, Benny?" he said. "You're really my own thoughts, so you'll be with me for the rest of my life."

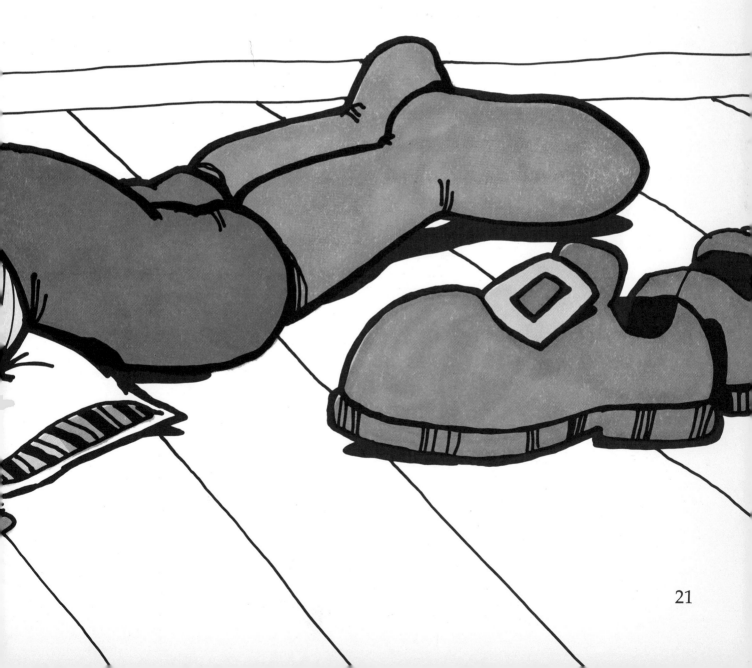

21

As you might guess, Ben went to the bookstore often. He was a friend of John, the apprentice who worked there.

"You know, John," he said one day, "I've thought of a way to read even more books without spending a lot of money to buy them. Of course I'll need the bookstore owner's permission. Will you talk to him for me?"

"That depends," said John. "What do you want to do?"

"I'd like to borrow books," Ben said. "I could read them after the store is closed and return them the next morning."

"I guess it won't hurt to ask," said John, and he and Ben went off to talk with the man who owned the bookstore.

The bookseller was a good-natured man, and he let Ben borrow a book that night. When Ben read it quickly and returned it safely in the morning, the man loaned Ben another book, and another and another. Soon Ben had read heaps of books without spending any of his savings.

"I've never been so happy," Ben told Benny as he walked back toward the print shop early one day. "Now if I'm lucky, I'll see some of my favorite people after I get to work."

Can you guess who Ben's favorite people were?

Why they were the authors of the very same books that Ben borrowed from the bookseller.

Ben's brother printed a newspaper, you see, as well as pamphlets and brochures and advertisements. Some of the best writers in the countryside would come to the printing shop to talk with James about stories for the paper.

Ben always managed to be working close by when the writers were in the shop. "There they are," he would whisper to Benny, and he would watch the great men. "Some day I'm going to be a fine writer, too, just like they are."

"You really *are* dreaming now," Benny said. "How can you learn to be a writer when you don't even go to school?"

"Don't worry," said Ben. "I'll find a way."

Do you know what Ben did then?

He took his favorite books—the ones he had bought and saved—and he read parts of them very carefully. After he finished reading a few pages, he would close the book and try to write the same story himself, or explain the same ideas. Then he compared what he had written with the pages in the book.

To be sure, the pages in the books were better at first, but Ben didn't get discouraged. "I'll keep practicing," he said. "Some day I'll write as well as the men who wrote these books."

It took a lot of work, but Ben finally was able to write very well. "Now I can make up my own stories," he said. "Maybe I can even write something for the newspaper."

But James did not like the idea of having his little brother write for the paper. "Forget it, Ben," he said. "You're too young. Nobody cares what you think."

How do you suppose it made Ben feel when his brother talked to him like that?

At first it made him feel sad. But when Ben told his friend John about it, John laughed. "Why don't you write a story for the newspaper anyway," John said. He had a twinkle in his eye. "You could put a funny name on the story. Lots of writers do it. Then you could watch James to see if he figures out who really wrote it."

Ben chuckled. "That could be fun," he said. And he and John and Benny had a good time thinking up a name to put on Ben's first story.

"I know!" said Ben at last. "I'll be Mrs. Silence Dogood, because it will do me good to keep silent." Benny and John laughed and agreed that it would be a good name indeed.

Ben went home then and wrote his story, and wrote it again and again until it was as good as he could make it. When it was finished, he went down to the newspaper office and put it under the door, where James would find it in the morning. Then he sat back and waited to see what would happen.

29

What happened was that James liked the story. He liked it so much that he printed it in his newspaper. Everyone who read the paper liked it, too.

Ben laughed to himself. "I'd love to tell James who Silence Dogood really is," he said to Benny.

"Better not," warned Benny. "I think James is already a little jealous of you. Don't make things worse."

So Ben kept quiet, and he kept on writing stories and leaving them under the door for James to find. Ben wasn't paid any money for the stories, of course, because no one knew who Mrs. Silence Dogood was. But Ben didn't care too much. He was still buying his own food with the money his brother gave him, and he was saving money, too.

But at last the day came when Ben simply couldn't keep his secret any longer. He told James he was Silence Dogood.

"You tricked me!" said James. He was very angry. "You watch out, Ben Franklin," he warned. "Don't start thinking you're so good!"

31

Ben couldn't please James after that, no matter how hard he tried. James often shouted at Ben for no reason. Sometimes James even beat his little brother with a stick. A master *could* beat an apprentice in those days, and there wasn't much anyone would do about it. Even Ben's parents couldn't help a great deal.

"I guess I've got to depend on myself," said Ben to Benny the penny. "I should. After all, I'm seventeen now."

"You'd better," agreed Benny. "*You* are the only one you can always depend on. Now what are you going to do about James?"

"I'm going to run away from him," decided Ben.

"I'm not sure that's a good idea," said Benny. "Be careful. I think James suspects that you might do just that."

Benny was right, for James went all over the city of Boston warning other printers that Ben might ask them for work. "Ben is my apprentice," James told the other printers. "He promised to work for me until he is twenty-one. He is not allowed to work for anyone else."

Ben was quite upset when he learned what James had done. "Now I'll never get a job here in Boston," he said. But the more he thought about it, the more he realized that Boston was not the only place in the world.

"Perhaps it's time for me to spend some of the money I've saved," he said. "That's what savings are for—so you have money to use when you need it."

So Ben bought a ticket, boarded a ship, and sailed away to New York. He didn't even stop to say goodbye to his mother and father. And when he couldn't get a job in New York, he left there and went on to Philadelphia.

But Ben didn't take a boat to Philadelphia, or a stagecoach, either. He wanted to keep as much of his money as he could in case it would be hard to find a job. So he walked much of the hundred miles. It rained along the way, and when he arrived in the town he was wet and tired. Just the same, a pretty girl named Deborah Read noticed him as he came along the street.

"Well, you don't look very good," said Benny the penny, "but at least you have some money in your pocket."

"I'm glad of that," said Ben. "I'll be able to get a room and have enough to eat while I look for a job. But I almost wish I hadn't run away. I broke the promise I made to stay and work for my brother."

That was true, and it would be many years before Ben and James were friends again. It would be almost a year before Ben went home to explain things to his mother and father. He felt sad and lonely as he looked for a room.

But after a hot bath and a night's rest, Ben felt better. When he went out to see the printers in Philadelphia, he found a very good job. In fact he now knew so much about printing that he was put in charge of a small shop.

Ben worked hard at his job, and over the years he kept saving. He found quick, easy ways to do things, so he saved time and work. He saved money, too, so that he would never be helpless and bound to a job he disliked.

Sometimes Ben saved money by doing things for himself instead of paying someone else to do them. The people of Philadelphia admired Ben when they saw him pushing paper through the streets in a wheelbarrow. "That Ben Franklin is a hard worker," they would say, "and he knows how to save."

Benny the penny laughed when he heard this. "You're doing more than working and saving," he told Ben.

What else do you think Ben was doing?

He was studying and reading. He was learning new things.

"We should all study more," the townspeople sometimes said. "If only there were some good schools nearby. But there isn't even one university in the whole Colony of Pennsylvania!"

"Then why don't we teach each other," suggested Ben, and he formed a learning club which he called the Junto club. He and ten other men met every Friday evening. At

each meeting, any member who had read a book or had otherwise found out about something told the others what he had learned.

"I like this club," Ben whispered to Benny. "We're not only learning about books. We're learning to speak well and to listen to other people's ideas."

By working hard, studying, and saving, young Ben Franklin began to succeed and prosper.

By now many of the ladies in Philadelphia thought that Ben would make a very good husband. But Ben knew that there was only one special girl for him. It was Deborah Read, the same pretty girl who had seen him trudge into town that very first day.

Ben had saved enough money to support a wife and family. And he owned his own printing business. He began to court Deborah.

When Ben and Deborah settled down to raise a family
together, Ben was always trying to find ways to make
their lives together happier and more comfortable.

One winter day, Ben saw his wife and children huddled
close to the fireplace. They were very cold—even though
the fire was blazing.

"We are cold," they said. "Most of the heat from the
fireplace goes up the chimney."

"I'm c-c-cold, t-too," said Benny. He sounded as if he had
little copper teeth that were chattering. "The fireplace eats
up so m-m-much w-wood, and it doesn't give back
m-much heat at all!"

"That's wasteful!" said Ben. "I think I can fix that."

Ben did fix it. He built an iron device which he called a stove. It was not like the stoves we cook on today, but it did get hot when Ben made a fire in it.

"It's really an iron box that fits inside the fireplace," said Ben. "It keeps most of the heat from going up the chimney. There's just a little hole in it so that only the smoke can get out."

"At last!" said Deborah. "The heat is coming into the room."

"It's nice and warm," said Benny, who was toasting himself beside the new stove.

"Wait until the neighbors hear about this!" cried the children.

When some of the neighbors heard about the stove, they said it was just new-fangled nonsense. They would have nothing to do with it, and they kept on being cold no matter how much wood they burned in their fireplaces. However, other neighbors did put stoves like Ben's into their homes and were snug and warm. And they didn't burn half as much wood. They called their new stoves Franklin stoves.

"Your stove saves energy," said Benny the penny. "That's what firewood really is, Ben. It's fuel, waiting to be turned into energy when it burns."

Today we burn gas and oil to keep warm. They are fuels, too, and that means they are sources of energy. Now it's even more important than it was in Ben's day to save energy.

Can you think of ways to save energy?

Ben not only saved energy and time and money. He saved ideas. He jotted them down on pieces of paper so that he would remember them. Some were ideas he thought of himself. Others he found in books. Many were about ways to save, and almost all were about ways to live a happier life.

"You should pass those ideas on to other people so that they can use them, too," said Benny one day.

"Now that's a great idea!" laughed Ben, and he began to write down all the ideas he had collected in a new kind of book. He called it *Poor Richard's Almanack*. It was not hard for Ben to write the book, because he had practiced writing so much when he was younger.

Benny liked the book. He especially liked the page where it said, "A penny saved is a penny earned."

"I'm glad you saved me," said Benny.

"I had to," Ben told him. "You're a special penny."

When *Poor Richard's Almanack* was printed it was a great success. Almost everyone read it. It was filled with good ideas and funny stories and wise sayings.

One of the sayings in Ben Franklin's almanac is really important today: "Waste not, want not." When Ben Franklin was alive, there was so much fuel and space and water that it seemed we would never run short. Today we know that we can't use these things carelessly or we will run out of them.

By

Benjamin Franklin

WASTE NOT

WANT NOT

Like most busy people, Ben Franklin never had enough time. As he grew older, it seemed that he spent too many precious minutes looking for his glasses. He had two pairs by now—one for looking at close-up things like books, and one for looking at far-away things like street signs.

One day, as he was trying to find his glasses, Ben realized that when he looked at far-away things, he always looked through the top part of the glasses. When he looked at close-up things, he looked through the bottom part.

"Benny," he said, "I think I've just thought of a great way to save time—and trouble, too."

Do you know what Ben did then?

He cut both pairs of glasses into two parts. "I'll put the part of the glasses I use for far-away things on the top of the eyeglass frame," he told Benny. "Then I'll put part of the close-up glasses on the bottom. That way I'll have two pairs of glasses in one. And I'll never have to hunt for the second pair again!"

Ben's new glasses certainly saved him lots of time. And when his friends saw them, many of them wanted a pair just like them.

The glasses came to be known as bifocals. And many people still use them today. Do you know anyone who saves time and trouble by wearing bifocals?

Ben was very successful now. He surely did not have to borrow books from a bookstore. But he remembered how it felt not to have books. "I'm going to fix things so that everybody can have books to read," he told Benny. And he began to talk to his friends about his new idea.

"Will you save the books you don't want any more?" asked Ben. "When we have enough, we'll collect them all in one place so that people can come and borrow them and read them."

"What a fine idea!" answered Ben's kind friends. And they gave Ben the books they didn't read any more. He put the books together in one room, and that was the start of the first public library in the United States.

Starting the first public library was only one of the many things Ben Franklin did for his fellow citizens. He also started the first fire department and the first hospital in Philadelphia. A school that he founded became the University of Pennsylvania. It was because of Ben that Philadelphia was one of the very first cities to have street lights. And of course we know about how he experimented with a kite and discovered that lightning was really electricity.

1ST HOSPITAL

1ST FIRE DEPARTMENT

1ST STREET LIGHTS

Ben's wife and children were so proud of him. His parents were, too. Even his brother James was happy when he had a chance to spend time with Ben.

Ben had time now—time and money—because he had saved when he was young, and he had used what he had wisely. He could travel to far-away places and learn new things and talk with different people.

Ben Franklin was so good at getting things done at home that he was asked to go to England when trouble arose between the king and the colonies. But even Ben couldn't solve the problems between the British and the Americans. So when the colonists decided to form a separate country, Ben joined others in signing the Declaration of Independence. And when our nation was very new, he went to France, where he talked the French king into helping us with money and other valuable things that a new country needs.

In spite of his fame and riches and success, Ben continued to find happiness in saving time and money and energy.

Because of Ben Franklin, many people today know the value of saving, so much so that many institutions like banks and insurance companies and even colleges are named after him.

Perhaps now you may want to think about what would make you happy. You may want to start saving things that are important to you.

Just like our good friend Ben Franklin.

The End

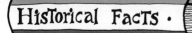

BENJAMIN FRANKLIN
1706–1790

Benjamin Franklin was born in Boston on January 17, 1706. His family was religious, frugal, and self-reliant. Bright, and eager to learn, young Ben was sent to school at the age of eight. But Ben's father, realizing that he would never be able to afford a college education for his son, took Ben out of school at the age of ten. It was then that Ben embarked on his life-long pursuit of self-education.

A common form of schooling in Ben's day was that of apprenticeship. And because of his great love for books, twelve-year-old Ben was established as an apprentice in his brother James's print shop. While learning the printing trade, Ben read every word that came into the shop.

In 1721, James founded a weekly newspaper called the *New-England Courant*. Under the pseudonym Silence Dogood, Ben wrote social commentaries for the paper that satirized Harvard College, criticized religious leaders, and promoted education for women. But James was overbearing and tyrannical, and he often beat Ben. So at the age of seventeen Ben ran away and left Boston. He ended up in Philadelphia almost penniless, but he was able to find a good job in a printing shop.

In 1728 Ben opened his own print shop with a partner. The partnership did not work out, however, and two years later Ben bought out his partner with money borrowed from friends. Ben worked day and night to save enough money to pay back his creditors. He could not stand being in debt and felt that only by hard work, thrift, and honesty could poor people release themselves from poverty. He was later to write in his *Poor Richard's Almanack* that "When you run in Debt, you give another power over your Liberty." First published in 1833, *Poor Richard's Almanack* was an accumulation of bits of information and old proverbs that dealt with industry and frugality.

Early in Ben's career, he brought together a group of tradesmen and formed a "club of mutual improvement" called the Junto. They met every Friday evening for discussions about how to improve themselves and the community. Ben and his friends founded such institutions as the first subscription library (1731), a fire company (1736), the American Philosophical Society (1743), a public academy for needy boys that later became the University of Pennsylvania (1749), and America's first medical center (1751).

Ben retired from the printing business in 1748 because he wanted to "read, study and make experiments." It was then that he began experimenting with electricity. His famous kite experiment in 1752 proved that lightning and electricity were identical occurrences. Many electrical terms used to this day were originated by Ben, who became known as America's leading scientist. Ben was also an inventor. The long list of his inventions include the lightning rod, bifocals, the static electric generator, and the Franklin stove—a heating device that made his home "twice as warm as it used to be with a quarter of the wood [he] formerly consumed."

Already a printer, publisher, scientist, and inventor, Ben turned to the world of politics and, in England, became the main spokesman for the American colonies. During the early years of America's quest for independence, Ben was dispatched to France to secure funds to help finance the Revolution. Ben was unique among our Founding Fathers because he was the only one of them to sign all four of the major documents relating to America's independence— The Declaration of Independence, The Treaty With France, The Treaty With England, and The Constitution.

Benjamin Franklin died in Philadelphia on April 17, 1790 at the age of eighty-four.

Other Titles in the ValueTale Series